COULD YOU LIVE IN THE PAST?

SHINOY AND THE CHAOS CREW

Contents

Written by Juliet Kerrigan

Collins

T0321642

Could you live in the past?

We're travelling back to the Iron Age, the Roman conquest and the Viking **invasions** to find out.

Timeline

Stone Age from about 800 000 BCE

Bronze Age from about 2100 BCE

Iron Age from about 750 BCE

Roman conquest of Britain 43 CE

Anglo-Saxon invasions of Britain from about 410 CE

Viking invasions of Britain from about 793 CE

Visiting Iron Age Britain

What were the houses like?

Large families lived in round houses with thatched roofs. The houses were dark inside because there were no windows. People slept on mattresses filled with hay, covered by rugs or furs.

reconstruction of an Iron Age house

This is what hillforts look like today.

Some houses were built inside a hillfort. Walls of earth were built round the top of a hill to keep people safe in times of danger.

What's for dinner?

Peas, beans and sometimes meat were cooked in an iron cauldron over a fire. Bread was made on a **griddle** or baked in a special oven. Stews and soups were eaten from wooden or clay bowls, sitting round the fire. There were spoons but no forks.

reconstruction of the inside of an Iron Age house

5

Where's the bathroom?

Experts believe Iron Age people used holes in the ground, with a wooden board to sit on – maybe in a little hut. There was moss instead of toilet paper and ashes from the fire were scattered in the hole to make it smell better.

People probably washed in streams or filled wooden buckets with water. Gritty food wore down their teeth. The only sweet food was honey, so teeth that have been found show few signs of decay. No toothbrushes have been discovered – yet.

What did they wear?

No clothes survive, but the tools for making cloth do.
The cloth was dyed using plants and berries.
People wore simple tunics, cloaks and leather shoes.
Important people had jewellery.

Chiefs wore gold torcs round their necks and they fastened their cloaks with brooches.

Were there any shops?

No – but there may have been markets. There were no coins until about 100 BCE, so people exchanged food, wool and iron.

When coins *were* first used, they looked like this.

Wheat, barley and rye were sown in the fields, harvested, and ground into flour for bread using a stone **quern**. Sheep and cows provided meat, milk and leather. Nuts, berries and mushrooms were collected and animals like red deer were hunted for extra food.

Did children go to school?

No one could read or write until the end of
the Iron Age. Children were taught crafts like pottery,
basket making and metalwork. They helped to look
after the farm animals. Girls were taught how to spin
and weave cloth. Boys learned how to throw a spear
and use a sword.

loom for
weaving cloth

Were there any battles?

Yes. Experts have found skeletons with injuries from
arrows, swords and spears. This tells us there was
fighting between groups of people.

Was there anything fun to do?

No, sorry. There wasn't much time for fun and games, but there were feasts at certain times of year – when the crops had been harvested in autumn and when winter became spring.

Some cauldrons found are so large, they must have been used to cook special meals for many people.

Iron Age large bronze cooking vessel

What happens if anyone's ill?

People in the Iron Age lived to about 25–30 years
of age. It was a tough life because there wasn't always
enough to eat and men often got injured in battle.
There were no hospitals or doctors, but people could
survive with a broken arm or leg. Herbs were used to
try and make people better.

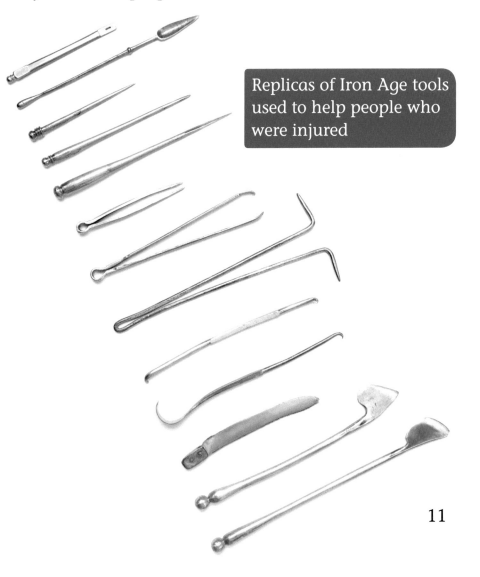

Replicas of Iron Age tools
used to help people who
were injured

Visiting Roman Britain

Why are the Romans here?

It was third time lucky when the Roman army invaded Britain in 43 CE. **Emperor** Claudius wanted to show how powerful he was by conquering Britain and ruling rich new lands.

There were soldiers from all over the Roman **Empire** in the army. They built roads and forts and tried to make sure the Britons obeyed Roman laws.

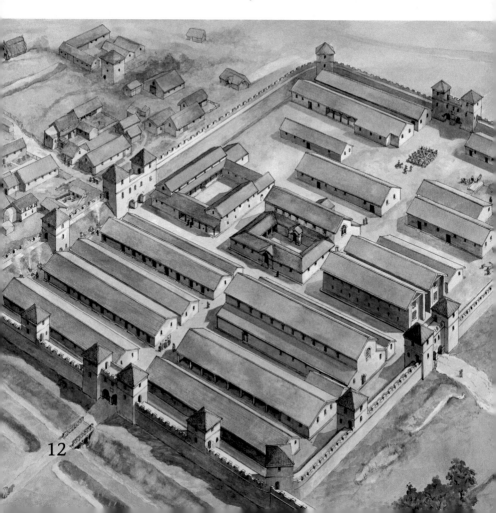

Did the Romans wash?

The Romans built public baths in every town. People went to wash (they used olive oil instead of soap) and to meet their friends.

Did they really wear socks and sandals?

Men and women wore wool or linen tunics. Important men wore a toga made of six metres of cloth – which is quite tricky to put on correctly. The Romans may have been the first people to wear socks with their sandals – Britain was cold!

Emperor Claudius

13

What kind of houses did they have?

Some people lived in the countryside in **villas** with small glass windows and **mosaic floors**. At night, oil lamps or candles were lit and underfloor heating kept them warm. There were wooden chairs and tables. Most villas had their own bathhouses.

Enslaved people did all the work: cooking, cleaning and keeping the fires burning.

reconstruction of the inside of a Roman villa

Houses in the towns were smaller than villas.
There were about 50 towns in Roman Britain.
Towns had a similar plan all over the Empire with
straight streets, sometimes surrounded by a wall with
four gates in it.

There were shops selling pottery, spices and leather
goods, and taverns where people could buy drinks
and snacks.

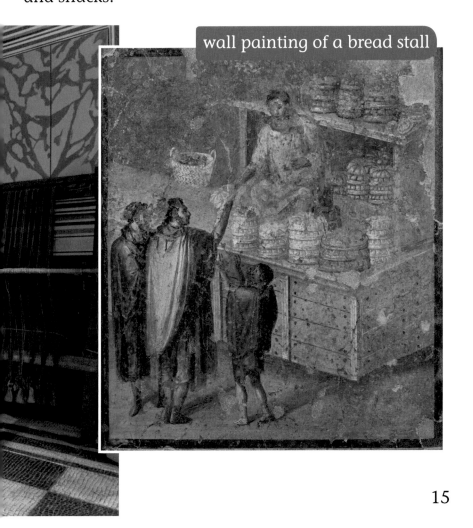

wall painting of a bread stall

What's for dinner?

At an important meal, guests would lie on couches around a table. The first course might be salad with eggs, followed by meat or fish, then fruit and honey cakes. They cut food into small pieces and ate with their hands. Roman cookery books had recipes for stuffed dormice and snails. The Romans brought new fruits like cherries and plums to Britain.

FACT
The Romans' favourite sauce was called garum, made from rotting fish.

Some food was produced on farms nearby, but olives, oil and drinks came in **amphorae** from all over the Roman Empire. These items could be bought with coins in shops in the towns.

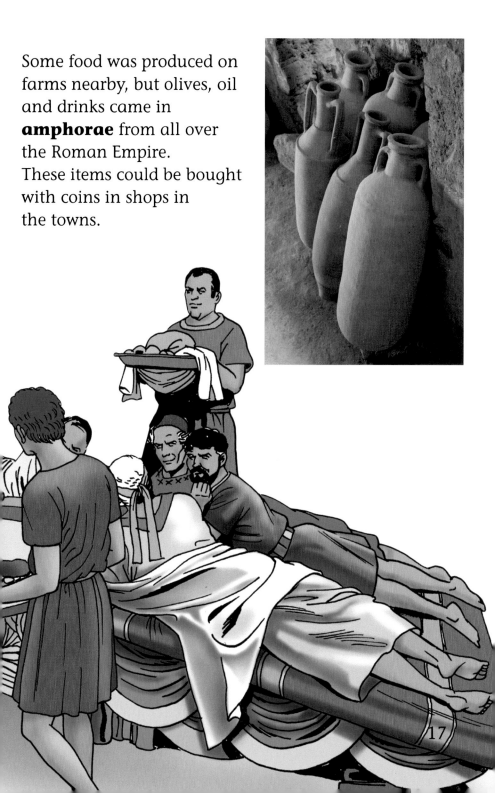

Are there any schools?

If you were a boy from a rich family, you might have had an educated enslaved person to teach you reading and writing in Latin. Writing was done with a stylus on wax tablets in wooden cases. A Roman tablet was *not* the same as a tablet you use today! Doing sums with Roman numerals was complicated, so they used a board with pebbles to help them.

Girls were taught how to spin, weave and run a household. Some girls could read and write. Poor children had to work.

What games did Roman children play?

There were balls and kites. Games were played with dice and knucklebones – like modern jacks. Outside some towns there was an **amphitheatre** for watching gladiator fights or a **circus** for chariot racing.

wax tablet and stylus

Roman checkers board

Amphitheatres in Britain would have looked like this.

Visiting Viking Age Britain

What are Vikings doing here?

The Vikings lived in Scandinavia. They sailed to Britain looking for loot and land to settle. Viking longships were up to 30 metres long and were given fierce names like Long Serpent.

Each longship was made of oak planks, fixed with iron nails, and had up to 60 rowers. They could sail their longships on the deep sea and shallow rivers.
The ships were decorated with carvings of dragons to frighten their enemies.

reconstruction of a serpent figure head from a Viking ship

Did Vikings wear armour all the time?

Not all the time, but the Vikings came ready to fight for what they wanted. They had round wooden shields, battle-axes and spears. Their swords had names like Fierce or Legbiter.

FACT
Viking helmets didn't have horns which would have got in the way in a battle.

What were Viking homes like?

Vikings lived in long houses built with wood and stone, with a thatched or turf roof. They had no windows and were dark and smoky inside, with an open fire to cook over. In the winter, farm animals lived at one end and families at the other. They kept cows and sheep.

What's for dinner?

No Viking recipe books have survived, but experts
think they ate stew with meat and vegetables like
leeks, cabbage and peas. Bread could be used as
a plate. They went hunting and fishing. At feasts,
a honey drink called mead was drunk from cow horns.

reconstruction of a Viking home

Did Vikings wear trousers?

Yes, boys wore tunics and trousers,
socks and leather shoes with
a cloak in cold weather. Girls wore
long tunics, with a shorter tunic
on top, held in place
with brooches. As there were no
pockets in their clothes,
valuable items like keys were
hung on a belt.

Archaeologists have found
razors for trimming beards and
lots of combs, but no toothbrushes.
Some Vikings decorated their teeth
by cutting grooves into them and
colouring them.

Did children work?

Yes. Children had to work and were taught crafts, like woodwork. Girls were taught farm work and how to run a household. Boys were trained to be warriors and hunters. Some people could write, using the runic alphabet.

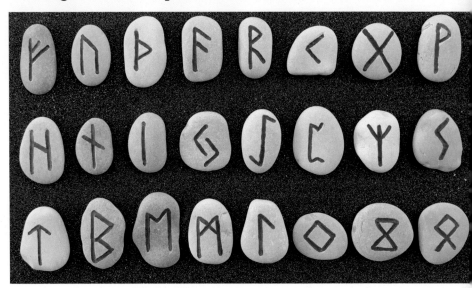

Were there any good Viking games?

Vikings played board games such as an early kind of chess. For boys, there were swimming competitions, wrestling, ball games and tug-of-war. In winter, they could skate on ice using bone skates tied on with leather laces.

a chess piece

On dark nights, families sat round the fire singing songs and telling stories about adventures, battles and heroes – maybe even a lost dog.

So, that's what it would be like to live in the past!

Glossary

amphitheatre large circular or oval open-air space with raised seating

amphora/e clay container/s with a pointed base and a stopper used to transport goods on board ships, such as olives and olive oil

archaeologists people who study the past by digging up remains

circus large open-air oblong space with raised seating

emperor ruler of an empire

empire a large group of countries with one ruler

griddle a flat metal plate to cook on

invasions going into another country, usually with an army

loom equipment for weaving threads to make cloth

mosaic floors usually patterned, made up of small, coloured stones

quern two stones, one on top of the other, for grinding grain

villas Roman country houses

Index

Iron Age

Roman

Viking

Same or different?

Was everything different in the past or are there things you recognise?

Iron Age

spoons (but no forks)

bread (with added grit)

pea and bean stew

fires

leather shoes

round houses

washing in a stream

Roman

stuffed dormice

rotting fish sauce

socks and sandals

writing on wax tablets

balls and kites

chariot racing

gladiator fights

washing with olive oil

mosaic floors

Viking

leek and bean stew

honey drink called mead

leather shoes

storytelling

ice skating

a sword with a name

wooden houses

coloured teeth

Ideas for reading

Written by Christine Whitney
Primary Literacy Consultant

Reading objectives:

- retrieve information from non-fiction
- be introduced to non-fiction books that are structured in different ways
- explain and discuss their understanding of books

Spoken language objectives:

- ask relevant questions
- speculate, imagine and explore ideas through talk
- participate in discussions

Curriculum links: History: develop an awareness of the past; Writing: write for different purposes

Word count: 1682

Interest words: quern, loom, circus, empire, archaeologist

Build a context for reading

- Ask children to share their earliest memories.
- Read the title of the book and ask children to discuss this question. What do they expect to read about in this book? Support their understanding of the word *past*.
- Encourage children to name three groups of people that lived *in the past*. When reading the book, children should check to see if their suggestions are mentioned.

Understand and apply reading strategies

- Read to page 11. Ask children to name five facts about living in the Iron Age. Which fact surprised them most?
- Continue to read to page 19. Ask children to explain to each other the difference between what girls and boys learned in Roman Britain. Was it different if you were poor?
- After reading up to page 27, ask the group to discuss the different education received by a boy and a girl in Viking England. Do they think this is fair?